United Nations Organization The Sorrow Of The World

Clever Fox
PUBLISHING
Chennai • Bangalore

United Nations Organization The Sorrow Of The World

Pitchai Gopalakrishnan

ISBN-13: 978-93-89113-44-0
ISBN-10: 9-38-911344-X

Published by CLEVER FOX PUBLISHING

CONTENTS

FOREWORD

The world believes that the UNO (the United Nations Organisation) was formed to stop wars breaking out amongst nations and to promote goodwill amongst them.

But the truth is that the organisation is an instrument for gobbling up unsuspecting nations without attacks, battles or incursions; ruin their individual culture, traditions, education and values; render them poor; and make them dependent for survival on the Western countries.

In what follows, I have explained the truth that the value of the Indian rupee and that of the American dollar is the same.

I have also explained that foreign investment is akin to throwing our own doors open for dacoits to enter, and the embassies of the NATO Nations are Centres for Espionage.

The purpose of this book is to assert that world peace will become a reality only when the UNO is disbanded and the 167 developing nations which are its members relinquish their membership in it.

This book is dedicated to the governments of the Third World or the developing nations of the world.

Irrespective of which religion one is born into, which religious practices one adopts, whether one is irreligious or a nonbeliever, the people of the entire world are guided by Hindu religious principles. I have elaborated this truth in the second part of my book.

PART 1
UNITED NATIONS ORGANISATION THE SORROW OF THE WORLD

1

THE ESTABLISHMENT OF THE UNO

Who Were the Nations That Established the UNO?

The vision and functioning of any organisation will depend upon the nature of the people who create it. When kind-hearted and compassionate people form an organisation, its vision and functioning will benefit people in many ways. On the contrary, if an organisation is formed by thieves it will only bring misery to the people through its vision and functioning. When an organisation like the UNO is established, obviously, its purpose would have been decided by the people who created it. If we probe into the nature of the countries which formed the UNO, we can get a sense of its vision and functioning. Let us take a look at the nations which were responsible for the formation of the UNO and also their individual characteristics.

The Birth of the UNO

At the end of the Second World War, America was the only country that profited greatly amongst the victorious nations. America had profited a lot by selling weapons. Also, the other countries of the world were compelled to use the American dollar. On the other hand, all the friendly nations like England, France and Russia faced loss of lives, loss of production and economic degradation due to the Second World War.

The European nations had occupied many countries of the world and enslaved them. But after the Second World War, they lost the capacity to manage these countries and to prolong their status as slave nations.

After the Second World War all the European countries faced shortage of even essential commodities. This resulted in internal agitations. European and American leaders had to control the internal agitations and also stem the tide of freedom struggles that were erupting in the colonies. The UNO is the brainchild of these leaders who feared that if they did not succeed in doing so, their own future would be in danger.

The UNO was the result of a plot to create an organisation which enabled European countries to keep the reins of control over the colonised nations with themselves and also continue to keep them as colonies.

When we consider the impact of the establishment of the UNO, we see that the European Christian nations which were embroiled in bloody wars and were sworn enemies for thousands of years have buried their hostilities of all those years, stopped engaging in battles and have been living in harmony for the past seventy-four years. These countries were known for their civil wars, terrorism, riots and struggles. But after the UNO was established, these countries have had no internal turmoil.

Contrary to this, the countries which never engaged in battles and were in harmony with each other before the UNO came into existence are now hostile to each other and are warring nations. The countries which never experienced civil wars, terrorism, arson and agitations are now exposed to internal strife, civil wars, terrorism, famine, hunger, starvation and economic degradation, which destabilise them.

Who Were the Nations that Created the UNO?

The UNO was established by the then American President Roosevelt, the British Prime Minister Winston Churchill, Stalin of Russia and Chiang Kai-shek of China. At the outset, France and another twenty-six nations joined them to form the UNO. The number of members continued to increase, and now 197 countries are members of the UNO. Let us learn more about the countries which established the UNO and are also keeping it under their thumb.

America

Those who migrated to America from various European countries slaughtered the locals and exterminated them in order to occupy their territory and called the continent America and made it their own country. Thus, the very birth of America is seeped with blood.

In the nineteenth century alone, America was engaged in 114 battles, which means it invaded 114 countries. Moreover, it is a country which tormented the Negroes through slave trade and even today tortures thousands of people in its torture camps.

When such a nation takes the initiative to establish the UNO, you can surmise what its purpose could have been.

United Kingdom

The Britishers are proud of saying that theirs is a country where the sun never sets. That is because they had enslaved almost all the countries of the world as their colonies. England was so merciless that it could occupy the countries of the world through treachery or war and plunder their wealth and make the native population suffer from famine, starvation and epidemics. England has always been indulging in one battle or the other down the centuries.

England had colonised South Africa and had been plundering its wealth and subjecting its people to endless agony till the year 1995. England has the power to veto, and using its NATO membership, it launches joint attacks on many countries of the world. And it was this England which joined hands with America to establish the UNO.

When the prime minister, Churchill, of such a country and the president of America, Roosevelt, came together to establish the UNO, what could have been the mission of such an organisation?

Russia

Russia transformed itself into an empire in the eighteenth century by capturing other countries and by annexing their territories.

It was in a state of war with North America, Central America and West Africa and with British India from 1750 to 1763.

Russia waged wars on Austria and Napoleon's France and also captured Finland.

Since the Russo-Turkish War of 1877–1878, the First World War and then the Second World War, Russia has been continually in a state of war.

After the October Revolution led by Lenin, a civil war broke out between the anticommunist Whites and the new soviet regime with its Red Army. During that period, the Bolsheviks and the Whites both had to face death sentences and exiles by turns. These events were known as Red Terror and White Terror, respectively. The civil war shattered the economy and the infrastructure badly. Millions turned refugees, and the Povolzhye famine caused the death of five million people.

Stalin put forth the idea of Socialism. The infighting within the Bolshevik party reached its peak during the Great Purge. The repressive period from 1937 to 1938 witnessed the death of lakhs and lakhs of people, including many party members and those who had plotted for a forcible change of government.

As the general secretary of the Soviet Socialist Party, Joseph Stalin exercised total control. During the years 1937–1938, he adopted a measure called the Great Purge by which he used violent methods, killed his political enemies and tried to establish his supremacy.

When Stalin was the leader in this scenario, Russia also joined hands in forming the UNO. So, what could have been the purpose of forming the UNO?

China

Once a nation of superior culture, China today has been attacked and subjected to occupation by many countries. Having lost its culture and tradition, beset with domestic chaos and battles, China today has a Communist face. Ever since China adopted communism, it has occupied its surrounding countries like an octopus.

Thousands of youth who demonstrated, demanding their rights and freedom in Tiananmen Square, were massacred by the Chinese government using military tanks.

It was this China which came forward to form the UNO. And the UNO has vested this country with veto power.

France

In the seventeenth and eighteenth centuries, France brought North America and large parts of Southeast Asia under its rule through immigration. In the nineteenth century and the early part of the twentieth century, France awoke to the greed for immigration, which was already impacting central and northwest Africa, South East Asia and many Caribbean islands. Next to England, France was the biggest nation of immigrants. Even this country has been given veto powers by the UNO.

When a country like France, which is known for its domestic dilemmas, civil wars and agitations, is a party to forming the UNO, what will be the nature of this organisation?

Dominate from Where You Are

What if a dacoit stops taking the trouble of going from place to place to loot and instead robs people by cunningly calling them to his place? Yes, that is what is happening now, and they call it the UNO!

Earlier, European countries used to undertake long arduous voyages, wage wars and use their soldiers, weapons and money to capture another country before they could plunder it. America and the other

European Christian countries wanted to avoid taking any trouble and find an easy way to plunder nations more without even letting them know that they were being plundered; the UNO was their brainchild!

The UNO is the outcome of a thought process. If each country goes about it individually it can rule over only those countries which are under its governance. But if America and the European countries come together to form a central organisation, they can keep all the countries of the world under their thumb.

If American and European nations occupy countries individually and rule over and plunder them, freedom struggles are bound to erupt and will have to be suppressed; one day or the other, they will have to exit those countries. But if they lure these countries through the UNO, there will be no freedom struggles erupting in any country, and they will never lose control over any country. They can keep all the countries under their control and keep plundering them forever. This was the idea behind the establishment of the UNO!

2

THE PRINCIPLES OF THE UNO

1. To enhance international harmony and safeguard the peace and security of all nations without resorting to wars.
2. To restrict aggression through collective action and each member nation is bound to respect the frontiers of neighbouring nations without attacking or encroaching upon them.
3. To resolve differences that may arise amongst member nations only through the international organisation as per international laws.
4. To respect peoples' equality of rights and the rights of self-determination.
5. To protect human rights and the fundamental rights of men, without distinction of race, language or religion and solve problems which may be of social, economic or cultural character.
6. To assert the sovereign equality of all its members.

7. To resolve the disputes of member nations through peaceful means without endangering international peace and security.
8. To provide weaponry to a nation if it is at war with a member nation that has violated these principles and engaged in war.
9. To not interfere in the internal matters of a nation under any circumstances.

3

THE STRUCTURE OF THE UNO

Principal Organs of the UNO

1. UN General Assembly
2. UN Security Council
3. UN Economic and Social Council
4. UN Trusteeship Council
5. UN Secretariat
6. International Court of Justice

The Principal Agencies of the UNO

1. Food and Agricultural Organization
2. World Health Organization
3. International Labour Organization
4. UNESCO (United Nations Educational, Science and Cultural Organization)
5. UNICEF (The United Nations Children's Fund)
6. IMF (International Monetary Fund)

7. GATT (General Agreement on Tariff and Trade)
8. World Bank
9. World Trade Organization

The First, Second and Third World Countries

It is essential to know about the First, Second and Third World countries in order to know more about the UNO. This is because some countries are making use of the UNO to strengthen their own countries and weaken some others so that they can rule over them. Many countries are being weakened by the UNO. Knowing about the First, Second and Third World countries will help you identify the countries which are strengthening themselves and the ones that are being weakened.

First World Countries

The Christian nations of Europe and America are known as First World countries. Hong Kong, Singapore, South Korea and Taiwan teamed up with the First World countries. As the First World countries were very supportive, these countries had to spend less on security and could increase their spending on development. These nations are known as First World countries.

Second World Countries

Countries like Russia, China and North Korea which are run on Communist principles are known as Second World countries.

Third World Countries

The countries which were colonised by the European countries belong to this category. Asian, African, Central and South American countries came together politically to form the Non-Aligned Movement. That is, they did not belong to the Christian countries of Europe or America, nor did they belong to the Second World Communist nations like Russia and China. Since its oil resources were completely plundered by the Christian nations, subjecting her people to hunger and poverty, Iran also has been included with the non-aligned nations, although she was never colonised by any country.

Big Brother Countries

Nowadays, instead of categorising nations as First World, Second World and Third World nations, the UNO groups them as developed nations and developing nations. It is just another way of saying that the First and Second World nations are developed nations, and the Third World countries are developing nations. The developed nations, which dominate the developing nations, can also be called the Big Brother nations.

The UNO's Functioning Is Contrary to Its Founding Principles

Problems and quarrels between nations have increased after the formation of the UNO. For instance, there is no history of India having waged a war with any other country before the UNO was formed, and there was no terrorism. It is only after the UNO came into existence that India's neighbouring countries like Pakistan, Sri Lanka, Bangladesh and China turned hostile. There was no Kashmir problem till the UNO was formed, but for the UNO, we would have never had the Kashmir problem. Similarly, terrorists enter India from all parts of the world, and within India too, Christian, Muslim, Maoist and Naxal terrorist groups are active.

The Chinese occupation of Indian territory, the Chinese aggression, three wars with Pakistan, war with Sri Lanka, massacre of Tamilian fishermen and border skirmishes with Pakistan, Bangladesh and Sri Lanka are all created by the UNO.

The UNO sees to it that many countries like India and Pakistan are in a perennial state of conflict. It makes sure that internal turmoil in the name of caste, religion, political faction, tribe, language or region always prevails in these countries.

Veto Power

The cardinal principle of the UNO is that all countries are equal before it. But it has vested America, Russia, England, China and France with the power to veto. Is this not contrary to their claim that all countries are equal before it? Imperialist nations and those countries which want to use nuclear power for their own safety have got veto power from the UNO. With the result, the UNO is hardly in a position to raise its voice against external aggression faced by member countries.

It is by misusing this veto power that America imposes economic sanctions on some countries without justification, ruins their economy and keeps them under its thumb.

Why Were These Specialised Agencies Created in the First Place?

If you give a cursory glance at the names of these agencies of the UNO, you would feel that these were created with the noble purpose of making good education and all other resources available to all its member countries.

1. Food and Agricultural Organization
2. World Health Organization
3. International Labour Organization
4. UNESCO
5. UNICEF

If you delve deeper, you will realise that the Big Brother countries rummage through every nook and corner of developing nations, destroy the traditions and culture of these countries and ensure that the people remain ignorant; they do it in the name of these specialised agencies. These are agencies designed to ruin the agriculture, water resources, forests and natural resources and cause famine, poverty, hunger and starvation systematically in these countries.

What Is the Purpose of These Agencies?

1. IMF
2. GATT
3. World Bank
4. WTO

A casual glance at these names would give the impression that the UNO created these agencies to bring about economic and trade growth in the developing countries. But in reality, it is a plot hatched by Big Brother countries to break the backbone of the developing nations by sabotaging the growth of their economy and trade, trap them in debt, and keep them in famine, hunger and starvation so that they remain dependent forever on the NATO countries.

If the UNO had created these agencies with genuine intentions, there would have been no poverty, no economic disparity and no hunger or starvation deaths in any country.

But we know how many people died of hunger and starvation in African and South American countries, and the ones who are living have either no food to eat or are malnourished and are mere skeletons.

It is because of the treacherous schemes carried out by NATO nations through the UNO that even in the twenty-first century we see poverty and starvation deaths prevailing in many countries across the globe.

4

WAYS THE UNO CRUSHES THE NATIONS OF THE WORLD

A nation becomes strong when it has economic freedom and growth. But the UNO continues to plot against such growth. A country faces more damage through attacks on its economy than through the ravages caused by a war on its sovereignty. The number of deaths caused by hunger, famine and starvation in the African, Asian and South American countries is probably more than the number of deaths caused by the wars in the Islamic countries of the Middle East.

These are the ways in which the Big Brother countries enslave countries of the world by weakening their economy.

1. Declaring the American dollar as global currency
2. IMF

3. World Bank
4. WTO (World Trade Organization)

Declaring the American Dollar as Global Currency

The respective currency of any one nation is not used while trading with other nations or for lending and borrowing money. Majority of financial transactions use the American dollar.

Therefore, it is America that determines the value of other currencies across the world.

By trading through a global currency, America profits in two ways. Firstly, when it buys or sells in dollars, it earns a sizeable amount as commission. Secondly, by undervaluing other currencies, America increases its own profit. When America reduces the value of the said currency against the dollar to earn profit, the value of that currency goes down in that country.

For example, if a country wants to engage in trade with America, it is America which determines the value of that currency. If the share market in any country crashes, the value of its currency against the dollar goes down. In this matter, the country in question has no say. Simultaneously, the value of the American dollar sees a proportionate enhancement of its value. As the said country has to use only the American dollar for its trade, it pays a hefty amount as commission to buy the dollar. In the final analysis, the countries that do these transactions hardly earn any profit. On the other hand, America profits tremendously through such transactions. When any two countries of the world engage in trade, it is America that ends up earning a profit! If this state of affairs has to change and the intervention of the hidden middleman has to be avoided, countries should relinquish their UN membership. In that scenario, the currency control measures of America will not impact those countries.

The Value of the American Dollar and That of the Indian Rupee Is the Same!

Indians themselves do not know the value of Indian currency. They start wailing the moment they hear that the value of the Indian currency is falling against the American dollar. It is ignorance that makes them wail so. Let me give you a few examples to help you understand the value of Indian currency.

In India you can travel in the second-class compartment of a superfast train from Madurai to Chennai, covering a distance of 450 km by paying Rs. 180, which is less than US$3. But in America or a European country, $3 or €3 is the minimum or first-level value of a bus ticket! In India, you can traverse the same 450 km in a second-class sleeper compartment of a superfast train for Rs. 315, which is less than US$5. But in America or Europe, you can go only up to the second stage in a city bus when you buy a ticket for $5 or €5!

Now you tell me which of these currencies has a higher value – the American dollar or the Indian rupee?

In a small village in India, Rs. 900, equivalent to $13, is quite sufficient for the food expenses of a family of four. In an Indian city, Rs. 3,000, which is equivalent to a mere $42, a family of four can sustain itself for a month on a reasonable scale. But $13 in an American village or $42 in an American city is barely sufficient for the three meals of a day! Now tell me which is more valuable, the American dollar or Indian rupee?

A packet of biscuits which costs Rs. 10 in India sells for $1.5–$2.00 or €1.5 or 2.00 in other countries – that is, Rs. 100 to Rs. 140! Now you tell me which currency has more value, the Indian rupee or dollar/euro currencies?

Here is another important fact: Indians who are employed in foreign countries are paid in the respective currency of that country. But they calculate the amount in Indian rupees, because the Indian rupee has more value as compared to their own currency!

The Indian government and business establishments which trade with America are compelled to spend the higher value Indian rupee to buy the American dollar which has a lesser value.

Contrast this with India's contract with Iran where we use our respective currencies for the transaction. If this system is followed in trading with all other countries too, there will be a rapid increase in India's prosperity.

Indians who trade with America hanker for the American dollar, unaware of the truth that the Indian rupee is more valuable than the dollar. When the value of the Indian rupee falls against that of the American dollar, they are elated. So they invest their money in buying dollars as if they are buying gold. It is because of such people that the value of the American dollar increases in an artificial way, causing damage to the Indian economy. Indians who are greedy for the American dollar should realise that the dollar cannot buy them even a cup of coffee from a roadside stall in India.

A tiger is powerful on land and an alligator in water. Similarly, Indian currency is powerful in India and American currency in America – let us be clear!

In the same way, the currencies of all countries have value in their own country. Their value goes down only when there is an attempt to convert them into American dollars, euros or British pounds.

IMF and the World Bank Loans

I feel that the two most fraudulent agencies of the UNO are the International Monetary Fund and the World Bank. Are you surprised? At the beginning of February 2019, I came across a news item. It said that Sri Lanka was to borrow 100 crore American dollars from China in order to expand the national highway from Kandy to Colombo.

This is a huge loan which Sri Lanka was taking from China. There are no Third World countries which do not take similar loans from IMF or the World

Bank. What is so surprising about these loans? The surprise lies in the purpose of these loans and the way the money is utilised.

We saw that Sri Lanka was to borrow money from China to build its highways. Similarly, many countries borrow money from the IMF and the World Bank for various purposes like laying of roads, building power stations, constructing dams or digging canals. If we were to raise some questions on these, we may get surprising answers.

Let us take the case of Sri Lanka's loan. We infer that Sri Lanka will expand the national highway from Kandy to Colombo by utilising this loan. Okay. From where will Sri Lanka get the land needed for expansion? The land is its own resource. From where will it procure the soil, gravel, cement, iron and other building materials? Again, from within Sri Lanka. From where will the labourers for the construction work come? From Sri Lanka yet again! Then what is it that China is going to give Sri Lanka? One hundred crore paper currency valued at one hundred crore American dollars!

Land, materials, building equipment and labourers are all available within Sri Lanka. When everything is available in Sri Lanka, why take a hundred crore loan in American dollars from China? This is typical of loans being disbursed by the IMF and World Bank. The countries that borrow may have all the necessary resources, yet they implement their plans by borrowing money from the IMF or the World Bank.

If you ask them, 'Why do you take loans from the IMF or World bank when you have all the resources in your own country?' these countries will tell you that they need money to procure land for building roads, buy construction materials and equipment and pay wages to the labourers!

A country cannot print its own currency as much as it wants. This will lead to high inflation. But if the countries print currency required for construction, to implement programmes for strengthening their infrastructure, there is no need to borrow from other countries, the IMF or the World Bank. Any loan carries with it the burden of repaying it. A government does not get any return from the programmes which are implemented by borrowing money from the IMF or the World Bank. Therefore, governments will find it very difficult to repay the loan with interest. At times the government may be compelled to incur another loan to repay the previous one!

The UNO, the IMF and the World Bank volunteer to lend money to many countries so that they are unable to repay the loan, are caught in a debt trap and are forced to remain under their thumb.

Therefore, if the global nations want to free themselves permanently from the debt trap, they should print sufficient currency notes to pay for implementing their programmes and improving their infrastructure.

5

LEADERS WHO GOBBLE UP FOREIGN LOAN AMOUNTS

The leaders of many countries exhibit a keenness to borrow money from the World Bank. That is because they appropriate the money for personal use without using it for the welfare of their countries. They deposit this money in foreign banks and live luxuriously for the rest of their lives. Leaders of the nation ignore the welfare of the nation for the sake of their own selfish interests. There are many such leaders in India, Pakistan, Sri Lanka and other such countries. Thus, all the money from foreign loans goes waste.

Foreign Direct Investment

Many world leaders including Indian politicians brag about the foreign investments they brought in as their achievement. Foreign direct investment (FDI) is nothing other than throwing our own doors open for dacoits to enter.

Foreign investment is also similar to loans from foreign countries or the UNO, the IMF or the World Bank. When we talked of World Bank loans, we said that what comes as foreign loans is nothing but paper currency and that all the land, materials and labour come from within the respective country. The story is the same in the case of foreign investments too. The difference between foreign loans and foreign investments is that a country has to repay the loan with interest whereas there is no such clause with foreign investments. But nobody seems to realise that foreign investments are far more damaging than loans from the IMF or the World Bank.

In the case of loans from the IMF, the World Bank or a foreign country, the responsibility of the debtor nation is over when the loan is repaid – albeit with some loss!

In the case of loans from foreign countries, the IMF, or the World Bank, the requisite land, building materials and labour come from the debtor country. Once the construction gets over, the infrastructure will be the property of the debtor nation once and for all.

In the case of foreign investments, there are special privileges given to foreign investors. The land for construction has to be given to the investor nation at a very cheap rate; what would normally cost Rs. 1,000 per sq. ft. has to be given for Re. 1 per sq. ft. Water, continuous power supply and raw materials have to be given at throwaway prices. They also get considerable tax exemptions.

The land that is sold to the investor country at a cheap rate will be the permanent property of their organisation. The host country will have to provide water supply, continuous power and raw materials to the investing nations for eons. Tax exemptions will also continue for years to come, thus making it a recurring expenditure for the host nation. After taking all these privileges from the host nation, the investing nation gives no concession to the host population when it comes to selling their products!

Do foreign investments increase job opportunities in the host country? No! The investing countries use automated equipment to manufacture goods; the host country does not benefit in terms of job opportunities.

When a nation incurs a loan from a foreign country, IMF or the World Bank, at least the loan amount comes to the debtor nation as paper currency. But in the case of foreign investment, there is no inflow of money in any form! In short, foreign investments do not bring any advantage to the host nation. On the contrary, the country that invests reaps huge profits. Moreover, they take these products that were manufactured at a very low cost to sell in other countries at very high prices and earn huge profits.

Foreign investment robs a country of its land, water supply, power supply and also taxes that are

due to it. All these constitute permanent losses to that country.

Countries give away land, water, power and taxes to the investor nations; instead, if they gave these facilities to their own people, it would be a great help to them.

6

COUNTRIES THAT HAVE BEEN DEVASTATED BY THE UNO

After the establishment of the UNO, countries are undermining their education, culture, traditions and virtues. Palestine, Vietnam, Korea and the entire lot of Islamic nations have faced havoc, and the process still continues. Let us take a look.

Palestine

There is no other country in the world which is as unfortunate as Palestine. England captured Palestine in the year 1918 and in 1948 created Israel for the Jews. Palestine was a land that belonged to Muslims; Israel was created and bestowed to the Jews over bloodshed. When the Palestinians protest to get back their own territory, the Christian world labels them as terrorists and showers bombshells over them. Israel is viewed as a favourite nation by the Christian world while Palestine is viewed as their prime enemy. Ever since Israel was created, there has been no let-up in the bloodshed in the Arab countries surrounding Israel.

All These Atrocities Take Place in Collusion with the UNO.

Vietnam

Vietnam was a French colony, and it defeated the French in a war and chased them out of its country. The Vietnam War resulted because of America's attempt to make Vietnam its colony. America needed a valid excuse to wage war against Vietnam and bring it under its own control; the excuse was to eradicate communism! America roped in South Vietnam, South Korea, Australia, Thailand and New Zealand for support in this.

At America's attempt to eradicate communism, Soviet Russia, China, Cuba, North Korea and Czechoslovakia joined hands with North Vietnam. North Vietnam became a playground for both the armies, and bombshells covered every inch of space in that country. America tested all its chemical bombs on North Vietnam.

All types of war crimes like rape, massacre of the citizens, terrorism, torture, murder of war prisoners, arson and destruction of property took place.

Who is America to eradicate communism in some other country? America likes to remain engaged in war with one country or the other all the time. Here is the list of casualties in the Vietnam War:

Vietnamese soldiers dead	11,00,000
Civilians wounded	14,90,000
Civilians dead	20,00,000
American soldiers dead	58,820

In the history of America, the Vietnam War was its worst defeat.

Egypt

During the reign of Hosni Mubarak, Christian churches came under severe attack in Egypt. Many died as a result of shelling within the churches. Therefore, America planned to overthrow the Hosni Mubarak government by using the Egyptian army as its puppet and bring about military rule in Egypt. America caused a military coup in Egypt and, within a span of eighteen days, overthrew the Hosni Mubarak government.

A reader might think, 'Why should the Egyptian army be controlled and bound by a distant land, America?'

Of all the North African countries, Egypt was the one with the maximum American influence. America gives $1.6–$2.00 billion as aid to the Egyptian army annually.

All the high-ranking officials of the Egyptian army are trained in America and have been brainwashed to work in America's favour. It is not just that. Egypt, Pakistan and many other Islamic countries have their high-ranking officials trained and brainwashed by

America. That is the reason a Christian country like America is able to cause military coups and bring about a change of government at will in Islamic countries.

The Egyptian army, which deposed Hosni Mubarak, did not rule over Egypt for long and brought about elections. Mohamed Morsi of the Freedom and Justice Party won and took over the reins of Egypt. America had not expected this turn of events. At the outset, Morsi was keen to retain his power and was supportive of America and Israel. On the other hand, he declined the friendly overtures of Iran. In the Syrian uprising too, Morsi was on America's side.

Morsi feared that this may anger his people and hence strengthened his relations with Islamic fundamentalists. He gave high government posts to the fundamentalists. He allowed repressive practices against women.

Morsi's ways were not to America's liking. It provoked lakhs and lakhs of rebels of its choosing to protest incessantly against Morsi. On the anniversary of Morsi's assuming power in Egypt, the Egyptian army deposed Morsi and appointed the supreme court judge Atly Mansour as its president and Nobel laureate ElBaradei as its prime minister.

Morsi's supporters started agitating all over Egypt in protest against these appointments. A state of emergency was declared to suppress those who were rebelling against the government, and the army unleashed tyrannical violence on the rebels. Thousands of Morsi supporters were killed, and thousands were injured.

ElBaradei, who was appointed by the army, resigned from his post in protest against their repressive measures.

America was worried about earning a bad reputation. So instead of helping the Egyptian army directly, it offered help clandestinely through Kuwait and Saudi Arabia. Its financial assistance of $1.6–$2.00 billion has now been raised to $12 billion, keeping Egypt firmly under its control.

Thus by controlling the Egyptian army, America is keeping Egypt under its thumb.

Syria

The civil war in Syria is continuing from 2011 till now because of the separatist tendencies encouraged by America, Saudi Arabia and Russia by instigating the majority Sunni Muslims against the Shia president of Syria. These countries have been providing military, financial and political support either in support or against the government or the military, keeping the conflict alive.

The impact of the civil war (some call it a mini world war), which has lasted for eight years, is as follows:

1. A UNO estimate says a minimum of 2.5 million lives have been lost.

2. The Human Rights commission of Syria has recorded the death of 3,46,000 people.
3. The number of people missing is 1,03,000.
4. An organisation has claimed that an estimated 4.7 lakh people have died as a result of a direct or indirect impact.
5. As per a UN calculation, 6.1 lakh people have migrated within Syria.
6. Nearly 70 per cent of the Syrian population is living in the grip of severe poverty. High inflation and food shortage have led to six million Syrians struggling to get food. In certain regions, people spend 15–20 per cent of their income to buy drinking water.
7. Approximately 7.5 million people live in regions which are not accessible to provide help.

Seventeen countries of the world are involved in the Syrian civil war in one way or the other.

America, Britain, France, Canada, Australia, the Netherlands, Saudi Arabia, Israel, Germany, Norway, Libya and Iraq are hostile to the Syrian government.

Russia, Iran, Turkey, Bahrain and Jordan are in favour of the Syrian government.

All the Islamic nations are facing a severe economic recession, and they are facing poverty as a result of the Syrian war. Syria has become a playground for the NATO nations.

Thus, all the wars waged by America against Palestine, Vietnam, Egypt, Syria and Libya and the resulting destruction have been happening right under the nose of the UNO. What does the UNO do to prevent all this? Then why do we need the UNO?

7

THE BIG BROTHER COUNTRIES THAT CAUSE TURMOIL IN THE WORLD

Islamic countries are agonised by Islamic rebels and Islamic leaders who are Christianised. Islamic leaders and rebels are pampered by Christian nations like America. They get carried away by this pampering, become puppets in their hands and are responsible for ruining the Islamic culture and peace in their respective countries. The Christian countries lure the Islamic leaders and rebels with gold, cash and women, draw them into the Christian culture and make them fight against the Islamic nations.

When Islamic leaders or rebels refuse to be lured by the pampering by the NATO nations, their governments are toppled by creating terrorists and rebels.

If you delve a little deeply or analyse seriously, you will see that the Islamic nations were never so much in conflict as we see them now and that not even 1 per cent of the population rebelled against the government before the formation of the UNO.

It is only after the formation of the UNO that in all Islamic countries and colonised countries like India and Nepal rebels and terrorists working against the governments were born. They were created by the Big Brother nations like America.

8

WHAT IS THE NEED FOR NATO WHEN WE HAVE THE UNO?

Those who believe that the UNO is working for maintaining world peace, safeguarding security and helping them develop should think a little. When there is an organisation like the UNO, why should the European Christian countries (except the Islamic country Turkey) come to an agreement and form NATO? If they have formed a powerful organisation called NATO, why are they still a part of the UNO? Why are they members of both the UNO and NATO? Here are the reasons:

1. The UNO should be an organisation which controls all the nations of the world.
2. The NATO countries want to share the benefits of the UN's dominance.

3. They want to use the NATO setup to make a joint attack on the other countries, subjugate them and keep them under their thumb.
4. NATO has been formed with the intention of imposing economic sanctions on the non-NATO countries and ruin their economy.

The European and American nations have a lame excuse for having formed NATO. That is, if any country attacks them, the combined military force of twenty-eight NATO countries will be their armour against such an attack. This can only be a cruel joke. How can other countries even think of attacking the superpowers like America, Russia, England and Germany? Will the idea of attacking even cross their minds?

There is evidence that the NATO countries work against the very purpose for which they were created. If one NATO country is under attack, it stands to reason that the other NATO countries should come to its rescue, doesn't it? Turkey is a member nation of NATO. And yet during the Syrian war and the Arab-Israel war, fellow NATO nations attacked it! In the Syrian war, if Turkey takes a favourable stance towards the Syrian government, America threatens to impose economic sanctions on Turkey. Thus, it is evident that the setting up of NATO was not to safeguard the security of its member countries.

The UNO makes use of the NATO countries like a rubber stamp to do its bidding in imposing economic sanctions against other countries and to subjugate them.

NATO Abolished the Non-Aligned Nations Movement

The NATO countries operate very intelligently. They have organised themselves as a group for their own selfish interests, but they are very keen that other countries should not form such a group.

Just as the Big Brother nations came together to form NATO, the Third World countries joined hands and established a forum called the Non-Aligned Movement to safeguard their own interests and to protect themselves from the NATO nations. The forum lasted till the year 1990.The NATO nations realised that if the non-aligned nations became a formidable force by including many countries of the world, they would not be able to subjugate any country. They made use of some flunkeys in the non-aligned group to create confusion amongst them and abolished the whole setup.

Had the non-aligned group of nations existed now, there would have been no war, civil wars or attacks from the NATO countries in the world, particularly in the Middle Eastern (Islamic) countries.

Sri Lankan Affairs

The Sinhalese and Tamilians lived in harmony till the time Sri Lanka became a member of the UNO.

But the moment it became a member of the UNO, they provoked the Sinhalese majority against the Tamilians and made the rulers of Sri Lanka themselves torture the Tamilians. On the other hand, they helped the Tamilians to form the Liberation Tigers organisation, gave them arms support and made them rebel against their own government. The NATO nations provoked a civil war and ruined Sri Lanka and its economy.

From Sirimavo Bandaranaike to today's Sirisena, all are toy presidents appointed by the Big Brother nations. Not one of them had or has the capacity to think on his or her own.

Tamil is the most ancient amongst the languages of the world. Tamil culture was acknowledged as the model code of behaviour for the world. Although the Tamilians who are in India have adopted the Christian culture, taken to eating meat and drinking and have forgotten their own culture completely, the Sri Lankan Tamils have preserved their language and culture and kept it evergreen.

With heightened awareness, the Tamil people created a warring force called the Liberation Tigers to fight against the Sri Lankan government, which was trying to crush them. If there is a decent warring force in the world, it is the Tamil Liberation Tigers. These tigers never attacked the Sinhalese public, the elderly, women or children and never indulged in rape or terrorist activities.

The Liberation Tigers directed their anger on the Sinhalese government, police and army, which were tormenting their tribe. The world has never come across a liberation movement which conducted itself with such discipline and righteousness. Nor is it likely to see one in the future.

The Sri Lankan government and its army could not even touch the Liberation Tigers who were intelligent and brave. Nepal is the only Hindu country in the world. The NATO countries helped the Maoists, through India, to crush the Nepalese army, topple its government and, through violence and terrorist tactics, capture the regime in Nepal. In Sri Lanka, the Tamil Tigers fought for the safety of their own people, but the NATO countries made sure that the Liberation Tigers were branded as a terrorist movement and made sure that they did not get support from any quarter.

To destroy the powerful Liberation Tigers and the Tamil tribe, the NATO countries used their puppets who ruled India—namely, Sonia Gandhi and Manmohan Singh—and destroyed the ship that was carrying arms for the Tamil Tigers by using very powerful Indian Air Force planes. They not only helped the Sri Lankan Air Force with money and weapons to massacre the common people but also decimated the Tamil Liberation Tiger movement and carried out a genocide of 4.5 lakh innocent Tamil people.

After having done away with the Liberation Tigers and conducting a genocide of the Tamil tribe, the

NATO countries and China have turned Sri Lanka into a debtor nation, destroyed the culture and tradition of the Sri Lankan people and are now plundering its natural resources. If the Tamil Liberation Tigers had continued to be present, they would have been alert to the fact that foreigners were looting Sri Lanka and would have stopped the plunder. That is why the NATO countries fulfilled their mission by using the Indian and Sri Lankan Armies.

Now, Sri Lanka has lost its culture, tradition and virtues. The Sinhalese people do not have the awareness that their country is being looted. The Sri Lankan president and the prime minister are fighting with each other for power and status.

Very soon Sri Lanka will join the ranks of Ethiopia and Somalia as a debtor nation, and it is going to be decimated through deadly famine, hunger, starvation, domestic turbulence and epidemics. This is going to be Sri Lanka's punishment for wiping out the Liberation Tigers.

The way the NATO nations helped wipe out the Tamil people in Sri Lanka is an example of how the UNO is an organisation that helps transgressors.

When India itself was going through an economic crisis, the Sonia Gandhi-Manmohan Singh duo spent crores of rupees to wipe out the Liberation Tigers and to massacre the Tamil people.

The Sonia Gandhi -Manmohan Singh duo who spent crores of rupees to massacre innocent people in Sri Lanka also spent crores of rupees to topple the Hindu government in Nepal. Crores of rupees can be spent by a nation for welfare measures, but in India, money has been spent for destructive activities in an irresponsible and arbitrary manner by Sonia Gandhi and Manmohan Singh.

Just like Sonia Gandhi-Manmohan Singh, the NATO countries have created puppet governments which dance to their tunes.

An example of this is the way the presidents were murdered in Iraq, Egypt and Libya, and puppet governments were established.

Iraq-Saddam Hussein

The turn of events in Iraq provides more proof to show that the UNO is an organisation that supports political manoeuvres.

Saddam Hussein was ruling Iraq very well. When the other Islamic nations were being ruled by the puppets of the European countries, Saddam Hussein saw to it that the NATO countries did not poke their noses in his country's affairs. He was aware that the European countries that dominated other countries could well try to do the same to him and his country; hence he enhanced the security arrangements of his country. If a country and its ruler are assertive, they are obviously not liked by the NATO countries. They put their heads together to find an excuse to attack the oil-rich Iraq and bring it under their control. They spread the hoax that Iraq was making atom bombs and chemical bombs and that it was hoarding these bombs. They took the UNO's help to send a team to Iraq to check if they had indeed stocked atom bombs and chemical bombs. The world was made to believe that the UN team went to check if Iraq had indeed stocked chemical bombs. But the UN team had gone to Iraq only to spy on it! That is, to assess the country's security arrangements, military strength, stock of weapons and where they were stocked. But in this spying exercise, the UN team could not find atom bombs or chemical bombs. Now they had to find another excuse to attack Iraq; they hit upon the idea of provoking Saddam Hussein to attack Kuwait. The otherwise shrewd Saddam Hussein got trapped by the NATO countries' ploy. The NATO espionage team suggested to Saddam Hussein that he could enrich his economy by attacking Kuwait which had no protection. Saddam Hussein's Iraqi army captured Kuwait in no time, not realising that it was a trap set up for him and his country.

Now the NATO countries had a valid excuse to attack Iraq! Without wasting time, all the twenty-eight nations joined hands to attack the Iraqi army in Kuwait and recovered Kuwait. The NATO countries should have terminated the attack here, if their intention was to recover Kuwait. On the other hand, the armies of all the twenty-eight NATO nations with different forms of weaponry attacked Iraq and caused irrevocable damage to that country. Within a matter of seventy-two hours, the NATO armies defeated Iraq in a war and brought it under their control.

The defeated Saddam Hussein hid himself in a bunker. The NATO countries found him and hauled him to the country's court. Any idea what the charges against him were? Not hoarding atom bombs or chemical bombs as you would think! The charge was that he was guilty of genocide of the Kurd tribe of Iraq! The aim of the NATO countries was to overthrow Saddam Hussein and capture Iraq. But the charges against him were:

1. Iraq had hoarded atom bombs
2. Iraq had hoarded chemical bombs
3. Iraq had massacred the minority Kurd tribe

Lies come in different colours, don't they?

A president rules over his country superbly. Rank outsiders come, establish that he is a criminal deserving the death sentence and hang him to death. Is this the role of the UNO?

At present, the NATO countries have appointed a puppet as president, and the twenty-eight countries are in the process of hurriedly robbing Iraq to recover the money they had spent in the Iraq war with interest. The NATO countries have converted Iraq into a dark nation without ever letting the world know how the people of Iraq live.

9

THE EMBASSIES OF THE NATO NATIONS ARE CENTRES FOR ESPIONAGE

Are you aware that the embassies of the NATO countries are actually centres for espionage? Every country thinks that embassies are meant for enhancing and strengthening relations between two countries. That is the ideal purpose of embassies. The UNO sanctions the freedom of foreign embassies to function with the full freedom of a nation. It is said that this strengthens the relations between two countries. Verifying the passports of people who want to go abroad, issuing visas to them and also safeguarding the welfare of travellers from their own country, who may be visiting the country for different reasons, is the avowed purpose of having embassies.

But the embassies of the member countries of the UNO, especially the NATO countries, use these embassies to spy on the host nation to carry out nefarious activities, to exercise control over the host nation and to occupy them.

What Is the Extent of Authority Vested in the Embassies by the UNO?

An embassy functioning in a foreign country operates with the full rights of a free country. The host country's rules and regulations do not bind the embassy. But the embassies can implement rules and regulations as they wish. The host country cannot intervene in anything that may happen within the embassy, nor can it take any action. A country should not spy on the embassies of other countries, nor can it intercept phone calls and e-mails meant for the embassy. The police or army of the host country can never enter the embassy. On the other hand, the host country should give full protection to the embassies.

If the employees or officers of the embassy commit a crime, the host country cannot take any action against them. At best it can complain to the ambassador – that is all. In the case of very serious crimes, the host country may expel them from the embassy – that is all.

If a country wants to spy on another, it has multiple hurdles. Finding a dependable spy and planting him in the other country is difficult. Finding the critical areas which are his focus is difficult for the spy. Gathering inputs from relevant individuals is difficult. Sending the gathered information to his own country is equally difficult. Nor can he receive information that comes to him from his own country. To cause damage to the host country by using the information is even more risky. In the event of a group of spies operating together, establishing communication amongst themselves is also difficult.

Embassies resulted because of the NATO countries' brainwave! As the host country is expected to accord the status of a free country to the embassies, NATO countries appoint expert spies capable of nefarious activities as their ambassadors in other countries!

These ambassadors live in total comfort, function without a trace of fear or worry and keep a close watch on the host country's economy, politics, security and lifestyle and share the information with the country of their origin. As per the directions given by their countries, they carry out destructive activities and cause political changes, domestic turmoil and terrorism. They instigate the host country to wage wars with other countries; they destroy the economy and resources of the host country.

If the NATO countries suspect that any individual might enter one of their countries and play havoc there, they keep a tab on them through the embassies and make sure that they never gain entry into their own countries; they refuse visas to such individuals and protect the interests of their own country!

Thus, the embassies of NATO nations in other countries happen to be places of impending danger.

It is not just the NATO nations; even enemy countries spy on embassies and utilise their services for carrying out nefarious activities.

Apart from spying through the embassies, the NATO countries make their way into the Third World countries in the name of freedom of the press. They conduct espionage activities and cause agitations in the name of religion, tribe, caste, colour and factions and indulge in destructive activities too. When the natives are not guaranteed freedom and rights, NATO journalists are given many rights and freedom – isn't this ironical? If the journalist of a NATO nation is attacked, the UNO considers it a major crime – in other words, if the host country forbids espionage activities, it is committing a crime!

The UNO Acts like a Licence for the NATO Countries

The truth is, the NATO countries use the UNO as a key that opens all doors across the globe for them and also bestows on them the right to attack or damage any country in the world.

1. The twenty-eight NATO countries destroyed Iraq in a war and hanged its president Saddam Hussein.
2. The NATO countries attacked Libya and expelled their leader Gaddafi from his own country.

3. The American army entered Pakistan to attack and kill Osama Bin Laden.

How can countries attack other free nations? Just think about it: Can we allow strangers to enter our homes with guns and shells, attack the inmates, kill them and loot what is available in the house?

But this what NATO countries have done in countries like Iraq, Libya, Syria and Pakistan. What are the relations between the NATO countries and the ones they choose to attack – either of friendship or of enmity? Nothing! Then why do they attack and cause turmoil in other countries?

The NATO countries and Iraq are far away from each other, yet the NATO countries attacked and ruined Iraq. If you were to ask them, 'What gives you the right to attack Iraq?' do you know what the reply would be? The UNO is like a family, and we are all members of the same family, and therefore we have every right to intervene!

Thus, the UNO serves as a licence to all the NATO countries to attack the global nations.

Licence to Kill

Do we need an organisation (UNO) which gives the right to some nations to enter any country, attack them, loot their resources and cause agitations? Certainly not!

Until about four hundred years ago, European countries entered another country to wage a war or to do business with it. They would undertake long voyages, discover a country, and enter it with the purpose of either doing business or spreading Christianity. They fought with the rulers and leaders of that country. They took many years to bring it under their control. In the meanwhile, they had to face competition with other countries. So, they fought wars with them either in the occupied country or in Europe, lost their money, their soldiers, dealt with the uprising that came up for freedom, finally enslaved them and ruled over them after a long-drawn struggle lasting many years.

But after the formation of the UNO, the European nations find it very easy to bring other countries under their control.

They need not undertake long voyages as before, need not bother to spread Christianity under the garb of trade, need not wage wars with competing nations, nor is there is any need to quell the freedom struggles of the respective countries.

Using the membership of the UNO as a licence to kill, the NATO countries brought Iraq under their control in a matter of seventy-two hours, captured Libya in less than a month, and ruined Syria within a few years; in the twinkling of an eye, faraway America attacked and murdered Osama bin Laden, who was in Pakistan.

After all this, they say that the UNO is an organisation which guarantees world peace!

In reality, the UNO is a trap set up to trap other countries or a dragnet to pull countries into its ambit.

10

DIVIDE AND RULE POLICY OF NATO COUNTRIES

European Christian countries (America, Australia and New Zealand are included here as much of their populations emigrated from Europe) spread Christianity to bring a country under their control. They not totally Christianised countries like India, in Islamic countries where one cannot preach Christianity at all, they used the policy of divide and rule. This also leads to hostility amongst neighbouring nations.

When the Christian countries occupy a country, they divide the natives on the basis of their caste, religion, tribe, language or political faction and make sure that they are in a perennial state of conflict with each other. Because of this policy of divide and rule, people who had been living in harmony so far end up quarrelling with each other and forget that their country is under the domination of a foreign country.

NATO countries use the same policy in Islamic countries as well. They create rifts between Sunnis, Shias and subtribes like the Kurds and bring about civil wars in these Islamic countries, plunder their resources and capture them. In order to make the tribes and subsects fight amongst themselves, the NATO countries segregate them sectwise, train each of them in warfare, give them money and weapons and also help them with plans to stir up turmoil.

To depose leaders like Iraq's Saddam Hussein and Libya's Gaddafi, who were extremely alert, the NATO countries provoked neighbouring countries to wage war against these leaders or brought these under their control through direct confrontation.

Christianity is for capturing countries and establishing dominance over them. NATO countries always keep Christianity in the foreground when they capture and enslave other countries. Does it mean that they are devout Christians, or do they have devotion and reverence for Jesus Christ? We can say categorically that it is not the case! You want to know why?

If the Christian nations truly had religious fervour with devotion and loyalty for Jesus Christ, what should they have done? In the European and American countries, 80 per cent of the Christians are not religious and only 2 per cent of Christians go to church. If these Christian nations really wanted to serve Christianity, they should have tried to attract the 98 per cent back to church and made them regular churchgoers. They should have worked for a Christian reformation in their own countries. But the Christian rulers do not take that path. People who are not successful in bringing the Christians in their own country to church try to spread Christianity in a big way in other countries. Why? Religion is a good instrument for capturing nations. Through Christianity, they cultivate loyalty towards the Christians of the NATO countries. By spreading Christianity, they make inroads into a country and capture it eventually.

It is possible to give further proof that the NATO countries have no loyalty to Christianity and that it is only a weapon for capturing nations.

In India, if someone so much as pelts a stone at a church, it becomes headline news across the world. The Christians in India condemn it as an affront on their religion. Not only that. Even for minor attacks on Indian Christians, you get statements condemning them from America, the Vatican, or even the UN secretary general. **But in China, nearly sixty-five hundred churches have been demolished in January this year. A law has been promulgated to say that buying or selling the Bible will be liable for fifteen years of imprisonment. China is banning Christianity. If the UNO, Vatican or the Christian countries had any concern for their religion, they should have conveyed their objection to China, shouldn't they? But neither the Vatican nor any Christian country is bothered about this; the UNO also has not pulled up China for this.**

The Christian nations or the Christian organisation never condemn the attacks on the Christians or the church. But in India, the reactions are totally different. Many years ago, when an Australian Christian priest who had come to India to convert people to Christianity was burnt to death, there were voices of protest from all over the world. In India, Bishops and Christian priests conducted protest marches for many years to condemn that death. Christian priests even today recall that death and provoke the religious sentiments of the Christians.

The Christian nations, the Vatican and the UNO turn a blind eye to the killing of Indian Christian fishermen.

No Christian organisation within India or outside India bothered about the atrocities on the Indian Christian fishermen. When Indian fishermen go to the Bay of Bengal for fishing, the Sri Lankan Navy opens fire on them; so far thousands of fishermen have been killed. The fishermen killed by the Sri Lankan Navy were mostly Christians. The Indian Christian organisations and Tamilian Christian organisations in particular never uttered a word in protest against the killing of fishermen. They closed the chapter by saying that some 'Indian fishermen' were killed. The loss of four thousand lives was of no significance to anyone; if the victim is an Australian, his being Christian is proclaimed, but if it is a fisherman, he is merely 'Indian'. This makes it very clear that the Christian nations do not recognise Indian Christians as their brethren. They look down upon Indian Christians who have converted to Christianity only to satisfy their hunger.

Christian organisations which protest to the state or central government for small issues like the demolition of a church never tried to stop the killing of thousands of Christian fishermen by the Sri Lankan Navy. They never submitted even a simple memorandum. Indian Christian organisations did not register even a feeble protest against the killing of Christian fishermen by the Sri Lankan Navy.

On the contrary, Sonia, Karunanidhi, Dravidian parties and organisations went to Sri Lanka and applauded Rajapakse for killing the Christian fishermen! The Indian Christian organisations did not condemn Sonia or Karunanidhi even for this.

The Indian Christians are orphaned both by Indian and global Christian organisations.

All Terrorism Points to America

In India, on 14 February 2019, a truck carrying CRPF jawans was attacked by a suicide bomber, and forty paramilitary personnel were killed in Pulwama, Kashmir. A terrorist outfit called Jaish-e-Mohammad, which operates from Pakistan, has claimed responsibility for the killing.

All the terrorist outfits operating in India, including the Jaish-e-Mohammad, belong to Pakistan. The world knows that conducting training camps for all these terrorist outfits, giving them weapons, supplying cash and helping them with their plans are all done by America.

The world knows that regardless of whosoever becomes the prime minister of Pakistan the real power rests with their army. All the high-ranking officials of the Pakistan army have been trained as well as brain-washed by America. Therefore, it is an open secret that this army is also under the thumb of the Unites States. It was Pakistan which helped America capture Osama Bin laden who was hiding in Pakistan.

A day before the terror attack on India on the fourteenth, a suicide attack was carried out on the thirteenth in Iran against their army. Iran accused the Pakistan defence establishment of having a hand in the attack. Iran has accused that the Jihadis of Jaish-e Adl supported by the Pakistani Protection Force was responsible for the attack on their army.

In another incident, a terrorist attack killed thirty-two soldiers who were sleeping in Afghanistan on 16 February.

If you connect the dots, Iran, India and Afghanistan, you will discern that America is behind all these terror attacks.

All Countries Should Relinquish Their UN Membership

All the countries of the world with the exception of the NATO countries and China should relinquish their UN membership and liberate themselves from it. Otherwise no country in the world will be able to enjoy freedom in the future. The NATO countries will write off those nations also. If the other countries resign from the UNO, the dominant nations will have no excuse to enter those territories.

If this step is taken, all the incessant wars of the Middle East Islamic nations will come to a close. The conflicts, turmoil, civil wars and terrorist activities will disappear.

The Developing Countries Should Form an Organisation Like NATO

If all the countries which resign from the UNO come together to set up something similar to the erstwhile non-aligned nations, a security setup and an economic agreement, there will be many advantages:

1. At present, only the dollar is the world currency. If countries can use their respective currencies, the dollar will lose its importance. The huge commissions that are shelled out to buy or sell the dollar can be saved.
2. When there is an economic downturn in any one country of the world, the other countries which are in no way connected also feel the turmoil. All the countries can escape from this impact.
3. We can put an end to Christians encroaching upon other countries, converting people and ruining the economy of that country.

4. In the absence of any interference from the NATO countries, domestic turmoil, civil wars, terrorism and conflicts with the neighbouring nations can be totally avoided.
5. The interference of NATO in every country's affairs will come to an end.
6. NATO countries will not be able to play with the economy of any nation or plunder its wealth.
7. NATO countries can no longer dump their war expenses or the expenditure on revamping a nation or other nations in a deceitful manner.
8. The practice of NATO countries of robbing the fertility of soil by using things like BT seeds can be stopped.
9. Every country pays money to the UNO towards its maintenance cost. This money can be saved.

Thus, by withdrawing from the UNO, no country will face any adverse impact; if anything, there are only advantages. These countries will progress rapidly without having to deal with hunger, famine and starvation.

There Will Be Strong Opposition to Resignation from the UNO

It is not easy for the Asian, African, Central and South American countries to withdraw from the UNO, because it is America which appoints leaders in these countries, makes them rich and pampers them. Also, it is America which trains the high-ranking army officers and other senior executives of these countries, brainwashes them and also pampers them. Therefore, these people will never agree to withdraw their countries from the UNO. In most countries, the people who are in power are those people who think, 'Let me not lose my luxurious lifestyle even if it means that the people of my country are dying of hunger, starvation or terrorism.'

Amongst the these countries, some have a prime minister like Modi who loves his country and does not fall for America's charming ways. Such people should resign from the UNO. When their leaders are unwilling to resign from the UNO, the people of the country should be able to bring pressure on the leaders to quit the UNO. All the countries of the world will be able to quit the UNO only when a leader says in his election manifesto 'If I am elected, I will see to it that we quit the UNO'. Such a leader should get elected if the Third World countries are to move out of the UNO's grip.

Some other countries may hesitate to move out of the UNO. This is because they may fear that the financial help and World Bank loans may not be available to them if they are not members.

There is no need to fear that the loans will dry up. Rich countries give financial help to poor countries, not out of compassion or an understanding of their needs. They give a small portion of the wealth that they have looted from the very same countries which are receiving the loans. If the countries are not members of the UNO, there is no possibility of these countries being plundered, and therefore there will be no need for UN help, loans and allowances! And as explained earlier, all the resources for development are within the country – what comes in as financial help is nothing but paper currency. The countries of the world should realise this.

A loan from the UNO makes a country remain deep in debt with the burden of the interest on the loan and never attains economic self-sufficiency and remains a slave of the UNO.

Therefore, all the countries can walk out of the UNO fearlessly.

Danger of NATO Countries Waging War

If the developing nations think that they can quit the UNO and live peacefully, the NATO nations will not let them. All this time, the NATO countries were living off the loot they got from the developing nations. With the military power, money power and arms power at their command, they will find some excuse to come together and attack the developing countries. The Big Brother countries will wage wars, ruin these nations and try their level best to keep them under their thumb.

How to Ward Off the Danger of Big Brother Countries Waging War?

Like the NATO countries have a military pact, the countries that resign from the UNO also should sign a military pact amongst themselves. As per this pact, if the NATO countries or China attack the country that has resigned from the UNO, the other countries should jointly provide military, arms and financial support. As per this, out of the present 196 UN members, NATO nations are 28 and the 29th is China. If you deduct the 29 from the 196, we have 167 nations. NATO countries can never withstand the combined might of these 167 nations.

The NATO countries with the help of military power and arms power may win to begin with. But because of the reasons given below, they will not get lasting victory.

The NATO countries and China have military strength, money power and arms power because they have been looting the less powerful nations so far. Once the countries move out of the UNO, there will be no opportunity to plunder those nations. Therefore, they will not remain powerful. The NATO countries will be unable to withstand an onslaught from 167 nations, and their defeat is a foregone conclusion. Because of these reasons, chances of the NATO nations waging wars are remote. Lastly, the non-UN countries have a trump card up their sleeve!

Returning Their Bitter Pill to Them

At present, countries like America, which keep the UNO under their thumb, make the other countries bow down by imposing economic sanctions on them. If the member countries wage war on any country just to subjugate it, the other 167 countries may impose economic sanctions on those countries. If the NATO countries stage a combined attack, economic sanctions may be imposed on all of them.

China as a Role Model to the World

When all the non-NATO countries were crushed and looted by the NATO nations, there is only one country in the world which is not in the grip of the NATO nations but has got veto power in the UNO on par with them. How was this possible for China alone? All countries including India and Islamic countries give free access to the Christian missionaries to their countries. But China does not permit Christian or Muslim religious people who try to convert people to their religion. Just by virtue of banning those who try to convert people into their own religion, China has emerged as a power on par with the NATO nations.

Very recently, in January 2019, China demolished sixty-five hundred churches because Christians used the churches for anti-China activities. It has also ordered the Muslims to accept Chinese culture totally within the next five years. That is, they are not allowed to identify themselves as Muslims.

China has gauged correctly that if Christians and Muslims are given leeway to convert people to their religious beliefs, Muslims and Christians are capable of stalling all progress in the country and ruin it beyond repair.

11

WHY DOES CHINA HATE CHRISTIANITY AND ISLAM?

There is a reason China has an aversion to Christianity and Islam. Just as they did in other countries, European Christians entered China as tradesmen, got them addicted to opium and spread Christianity. In the process, they ruined the culture which was as superior as Indian culture; they ruined the traditions and virtues of Chinese culture.

Blaming China for obstructing their trade, the European Christians attacked the weaponless China with their own guns and tanks, scattered them, occupied China and made China into a weak nation. Just before this, Islamic invaders like Genghis Khan had caused tremendous losses to China.

Repeated attacks from Christian and Muslim invaders had made China a weak nation. Many other countries of the world too invaded China and contributed towards devastating China. With the result,

China was unable to win any war till the Second World War. In the Second World War, China joined the Allied nations and tasted victory for the first time.

Then came the Communist rulers. They realised that the Christians and Muslims were responsible for damaging China irreparably and decided never to allow their country to be dominated by them; with this objective in mind, they banned all religions in their country.

China, with its experience of more than a century in dealing with Christians and Muslims, had understood that if these people are given an inch they would take a mile; they would decide China's fate and lifestyle. China hates these two religions like poison and hence the ban on these two religions.

Following the footsteps of China, India and other developing nations too should ban Christian and Muslim religions.

American President Trump Planning to Withdraw from NATO

American president Trump is planning to withdraw from NATO. Americans are objecting to this move. But why would Trump plan to move out of NATO?

America is the front-runner in planning attacks and carrying out the attacking on any country. It is America that lures leaders of other countries with territory, gold and women. It is America that lures high-ranking officers of all countries. It is America that pays for the training, finance, weaponry and plans of all terrorist outfits in the world. At times, the other NATO countries provide military support to America in attacking a country.

Therefore, Trump wonders why the NATO countries should be given a share of the resources acquired by plundering the occupied nation. If he moves out of NATO, America alone can enjoy the loot from the occupied countries without having to share it with other NATO members. Perhaps he is justified in thinking so! American public who cannot think ahead like Trump are objecting to the move.

The UNO Is an Inadequate, Useless Organisation

Where is Venezuela, where is India and where is America? The speaker of the Venezuelan Parliament declared himself as the president of Venezuela. But the elected president refused to step down. Countries like America recognised the speaker who declared himself as president. The fact that the elected president refused to step down angered America, and it imposed economic sanctions against Venezuela. Yes, America was upset, and so it imposed economic sanctions, but who is America to command other nations to follow suit?

As America has imposed economic sanctions on Venezuela, its economy is in the doldrums. Venezuela is requesting countries like India to buy its crude oil. But America has threatened that if India or any other country dares to buy crude oil from Venezuela, it is not going to be a mute spectator.

So according to America, the people of a country do not have the right to choose their president, but the world has to recognise the president appointed by America!

In a situation like this, what would one expect the UNO to do? America is not allowing elected governments to function. The UNO should request all the countries of the world to impose economic sanctions against America and make sure that it is implemented. If the UNO takes such a step, will America ever interfere in the affairs of every nation? Never!

The World Is in Danger with Every Continuing Minute of the UNO

As the NATO nations are forever taking the support of the UNO to plunder other countries, interfere in their internal affairs, provoke civil wars, patronise terrorism and instigate nations to be in conflict with their neighbours, every minute of the UNO's continued existence is dangerous for the world.

The moment the UNO is disbanded or the moment the 167 member countries (developing countries) withdraw membership from it, there will be no more wars, aggression or terrorism in the world, and peace will prevail everywhere – this is the Gospel truth!

Modi's Role in Ensuring World Peace

Had the abandoned Non-Aligned Movement continued to exist till today, there would have been no wars, civil wars or aggression from NATO countries on the Asian and Middle East Islamic countries. The Indian prime minister Modi should realise this truth and revive the Non-Aligned Movement. Just as NATO was formed by bringing together the 167 developing nations, the developing countries should come together to form an organisation. India should take its leadership and establish peace and harmony in the world. Apart from Modi, no other world leader has the ability or the zest to be at the helm of such an organisation.

PART 2
FOR PERMANENT WORLD PEACE

1

CHRISTIANITY-ISLAM – A COMPARATIVE STUDY

Christianity claims that it is the true religion and that its God is supreme. They believe that all other religions and their Gods are false.

Islam also claims that it is the true religion, its God is supreme and all other religions and their Gods are false.

Therefore, both these religions are taking measures to spread their respective religions across the globe ever since their religions came into existence.

But the Hindus never claim that theirs is the only true religion, their Gods are real and all the other religions and their Gods are false.

If Christians and Muslims claim that their religion is sacred and that their God is real and Hindus make no such claims, how do we know which is the true religion? We can compare them. It is by comparing the tenets of these religions that we can explain to the masses which is the true religion. Shall we compare these religions now?

Christians believe that love, compassion, pity and mercy were given to man for his upliftment, but they hunt animals and kill them for food; they show the same lack of love, compassion, pity or mercy when they invade other countries, grab their land and resources and torture the natives. All these are not humane qualities.

The lechery of the Christian priests transcends all distinctions of male, female, children, elderly, orphans and the crippled. These are not humane qualities either.

Whichever country Christianity sets foot in, immorality, turmoil, hatred and terrorism reside permanently. To sum up, Christians and humane qualities do not go together.

According to the Christians and Muslims, their Gods claim to be the true Almighties, and they bestow their grace only on those who have faith in them and not on non-believers. The Christian and Muslim Gods do not forbid the use of violent methods to spread these religions.

A Divine Being who blesses only those who follow Him or who refuses to bless anyone who does not follow His path – can He be accepted as the Supreme Being by the entire creation?

If you accept that Jesus is real, you also have to accept that Islam's Allah is not real. If you accept that

Islam's Allah is real, it negates the claim that Jesus is real. So the Christian doctrines do not acknowledge Allah, and the Islamic doctrines do not acknowledge Jesus. So both are unreal Gods! God creates all creatures, protects them and is worshipped by all. By this yardstick, Jesus Christ whom the Christians worship does not protect Muslims, and Allah whom the Muslims worship does not care for the Christians. Muslims do not acknowledge Jesus as God, and similarly Christians do not acknowledge Allah as God. Doesn't it follow that both these Gods are not real?

What does Christianity say? Jesus protects only those who accept Him as God. But Muslims, followers of other religions and atheists lead a better life than the Christians. Both in Islamic countries and non-Islamic countries, it rains, rivers flow and the bounty of nature is available to them too. Doesn't life continue in a natural rhythm of births and deaths?

What does Islam say? Allah protects only those who accept Him as God. But Christians, followers of other religions and atheists lead a better life than the Muslims. Both in Christian countries and non-Christian countries, it rains, rivers flow and the bounty of nature is available to them too. Doesn't life continue in a natural rhythm of births and deaths?

If that is so, the biblical saying or the Koranic claim that Jesus and Allah save only those who have faith in Him and those who worship Him must be false, shouldn't it?

We must realise that Hinduism and Hindu Gods are true. In the Hindu Vedas, God does not differentiate between one man and another. In Hinduism, God protects even atheists with love and care as His own children. Hence, Christians, Muslims, atheists and even those who belittle Hindu Gods lead a good life.

The universe came into existence many eons ago. But Jesus's birth dates back to two thousand years. Nabi, who conceptualised Allah, was born three hundred years after Jesus. How can we ascribe the creation of the universe, the elements, living beings, which have existed for eons, to a God of such recent origin? Doesn't anybody realise that it is illogical?

Whom did Christians worship till Jesus was born two thousand years ago?

Why didn't people who lived two thousand years ago worship Jesus? Think a little, Christians!

Similarly, whom did the Muslims worship before Nabi was born? Why didn't people who lived two thousand years ago worship Allah? Think a little, Muslims!

People who never worshipped either Jesus or Allah also had been inhabiting the earth for lakhs and lakhs of years. Who created and protected them?

Even today there are millions of people across the world who neither acknowledge nor worship Jesus or Allah. Can anyone tell us who created and protected them?

2

THERE IS MATERIAL EVIDENCE AVAILABLE ABOUT HINDU GODS

In contrast to all these, the Hindu Vedas contain chronological evidence to prove that the practice of worshipping Gods existed from time immemorial. The Hindu religion calculates the passage of time meticulously in 'yugas'. As per this calculation, the period of the Ramayana was seventeen lakh years ago. The bridge constructed by Lord Rama exists even today as proof that the legendary episodes of the Ramayana actually took place.

The Mahabharata took place nearly five thousand years ago. Dwarka ruled by Lord Krishna is submerged under the sea and is proof that the Mahabharata actually took place.

Mount Kailasa, which erupted on its own, is worshipped by Hindus as a manifestation of Lord Siva is in the Himalayan ranges. These ranges are as old as the universe itself.

In the very same Himalayan ranges, in the Amarnath cave, Lord Siva manifests Himself in the shape of an ice linga. This happens every year from the month of May to August without fail.

There are many parts of the world where manifestations of Hindu Gods have taken place.

Can the Christians and Muslims give us even an iota of evidence to prove the existence of their Gods?

God's Power to Protect

The year 2005 saw the occurrence of a Tsunami in Tamil Nadu. It destroyed completely the sacred Velankanni church of the Christians in Tamil Nadu. More than five thousand Christians who had gone there to celebrate Christmas were killed. Similarly, the sacred Nagoor Dharga of the Muslims also was affected by the Tsunami.

But in places like Rameswaram, Tiruchendur and Kanyakumari, where there are Hindu temples, the ocean receded, leaving the temples intact!

The whole of Nepal was destroyed in an earthquake. But the Pasupathinath temple and the Narayana temple in Kathmandu remained without a trace of damage.

In the year 2013, in the state of Himachal Pradesh in India, the whole town of Kedarnath was devastated by torrential rains. But the sacred shrine of the Hindus, the Kedarnath temple, was safe despite the fact that the area was inundated on both sides of the temple.

This is clear proof to the world that Hindu Gods are real.

The Hindu Vedas, scriptures and epics emanated from God. But the Bible was not created even by Jesus Christ; his eleven disciples created it. The Koran was written by the Nabi. All these were men.

In Hinduism, tips on how to lead a life and a code of conduct were given to man through the Vedas by God. But the Bible and the Koran were written by men.

Since God created the Vedas in Hinduism, there is no discord. But in Christianity and Islam, since the scriptures were created by men, there are contradictions. Both the religions claim that only their God is real. Yet both the religions say that God is one. If that is true, how can there be two different Gods – one for Islam and one for Christianity?

Understand that the Bible and the Koran were created to suit the lifestyle of people.

The Lord as a Role Model for Man

In Hinduism, the Lord did not just stop at creating the Vedas. He came down to earth as incarnations again and again to show men how to live a life guided by the Vedas.

That is how Lord Rama is an incarnation of Mahavishnu. Through this incarnation, the Lord exemplifies parent-child relationship, a child's respect for his parents, obeying one's parents, devotion to one's Guru, what is ideal bonding between brothers, husband-wife relationship, relationship with friends, the parameters of devotion and never to lust for another man's wife.

God in His incarnation as Rama showed the ideal way to lead a life and made His subjects emulate Him. Lord Ram as the king of an empire showed the world how to be an ideal king and how a kingdom should be governed through His *Ramarajya.*

When vices started becoming predominant and powerful, God established the triumph of good over evil in His incarnation as *Krishna.* He donned the mantle of a humble charioteer. He exemplified the way a diplomat should conduct himself. And finally, He gave the world the Bhagavad Gita, which tells man how to remain undeterred under all circumstance.

The Ramayana and the Mahabharata deserve to be discussed in detail. But the purview of this book and the time at my disposal are limited; therefore, I have condensed the matter to fall within the purview of this book.

But the Holy Spirit worshipped by the Christians and Allah worshipped by the Muslims are said to be gracing the world from their heavenly abode. So their feet never touch this earth. They have never shown men and women the ideal way to lead a life. When men and women are incapable of following the ideal path even when they see a living role model, how can we expect that they will be able to interpret and follow teachings that come from heaven?

The Hindu Gods always came down to earth in response to the fervent prayers from their devotees. When vices prevailed on earth, they came down to earth to destroy evil and establish virtues.

But in Christianity and Islam, God never came down but sent His angels, Jesus Christ and Mohammad Nabi. Why do the Christian and Islamic Gods shy away from meeting men and women on earth? Why do they need middlemen?

Devotion is bonding between God and man. Why do we need priests in churches and imams in mosques? Think for a moment, if God would ever think of protecting His flock through a middleman.

You may ask me, 'There are priests in Hindu temples too.' The job of the priests in Hindu temples is limited to giving the deity a holy bath, decorate the idol with flowers and garlands and carry on the daily rituals of worship. It is not authorised by any *Veda* that a priest can accept money from people for performing archanas, distribute the holy ash and holy water, mitigate the effects of evil spirits and suggest remedial measures to devotees. A section of society has established these wrong practices to earn an income for themselves.

The Christian religion has one scripture called the Bible, and the Muslims have one scripture called the Koran. But the Hindu religious scripture is related to the four main Vedas – namely, *Rig, Yajur, Saama and Atharva* and countless *puranas, epics, shastras* and devotional treatises, which lay down a code of conduct for man.

The Hindu Religion as Code of Behaviour for all Aspects of Man's Life

Every man is bound to be ill at some time or the other. Therefore, the God bestowed a medical treatise which is bifurcated into *Ayurveda* and *Sidha* medicines. Man's next need is a house to live in. The *Vaastu Sastra* teaches man what aspects of a house make it good for living. In order for man to know his present and future, the Gods gave us the *Jyotish Sastra.* We have treatises on astronomy, music, sculpture, painting and dance – a shastra for each of these. Why, we have a *Kama Sastra* which depicts true love and a harmonious relationship between man and woman. The *Garuda Purana* helps man shape his afterlife also well. Every human being should read the *Garuda Purana.* Reading this treatise will put an end to the sins that are committed in this world; justice, fair play and virtues will prevail in the world. Thus, the Hindu religion shows the path for all facets of a man's life. But other religions are incapable of providing satisfactory answers to any of man's doubts or needs. Thus, the Hindu religion has attained perfection from every angle.

Religious Structure Is Also like Party Structure

It goes without saying that Christianity, Islam and even Judaism, Buddhism and Jainism are all religions created by men. Christianity and Islam are like the Communist Party, with a few guiding principles. The Communist Party aims to capture other nations and rule over them. The only difference is that the Communists do not worship those who established the Communist Party or those who laid down its tenets. But the Christians and Muslims worship those who gave birth to their religion. It is not an exaggeration to say that the Bible and the Koran are similar to the Communist Party's rules and implementations.

It is further possible to establish that Christianity and Islam are hoaxes. Both these religions depict God as a Being who forgives all sins, grants every wish of a man and cures all ailments.

But the Hindu religion does not make such claims. Man should never commit sins; if he does, God punishes him by giving him problems, illnesses and accidents. That is the truth. Men and women face many problems because of their greed. They are always subjected to worries, miseries, fear, diseases, accidents, terrorism and wars. They get killed, commit suicides. More than anything else, they die due to earthquakes, tsunami, drought, famine, floods, typhoons, cyclones, rain, heat or snowfall.

Are Christians exempted from these miseries?

Are Muslims exempted from these agonies?

No!

How much ever they may kneel down and pray for forgiveness, they do not get relief from all these miseries. So their claim that God forgives all the sins committed by man is false!

If it is true that Jesus Christ and Allah forgive all your sins, protect you from all your sins, give you all the wealth that you desire and grant all the boons you ask for, why do you suffer at all? Why do you fall ill, live in poverty, live in fear, meet with accidents, commit suicides, get killed, get killed in terrorist attacks, wars and bombing? Why do you die of earthquakes, tsunami, droughts, famine, floods, typhoons, cyclones, rain, heat and snowfall?

3

SIN INVITES PUNISHMENT

What is the definition of sin? Going against humanitarian principles is sin. To understand what humanitarian principles are, one has to read the Hindu Vedas and religious treatises. Does it mean all the Hindus in India read these treatises and adhere to humanitarian principles? No. Since people have been following the *Vedic* pattern of life for eons, humanitarian values are ingrained in them right from birth. But the people of other countries do not have humanitarian values in their blood. Therefore, they should read the Hindu Vedas, puranas and religious treatises to know about these values.

Hinduism considers the eating of meat or drinking of alcohol as sins. Many Hindus are influenced by Christianity and are given to meat eating, drinking and immoral ways. With the result, they are afflicted by diseases, face problems in life, commit suicide, are murdered and die in accidents. We have to face the punishments for the sins we commit at the appropriate time and in appropriate measure. As long as people knew these rules, no one drank liquor in India, no one ate meat and did not resort to immoral ways. Therefore, there were no problems in the country, no diseases, accidents, murder, dacoity or suicides. But the influence of Christianity has made Indians lose their discretion and commit sins and experience devastation.

Christians and Muslims do not have a peaceful life right from birth. They lead a life beset with wars, murders, bombing, terrorist attacks, gunfire, accidents, earthquakes, floods, snow, drought, famine and starvation.

The reason for all this is that they have been committing the sins of drinking, meat eating and immoral activities for ages. They may think that the Bible does not say that these are sins. Similarly, the Muslims also may think that the Koran does not say that eating meat eating is a sin or a man having multiple wives is a sin.

The Sins and Virtues of the World Are Determined by the Hindu Vedas

All the people of this world, whatever religion they belong to, or whether they are atheists, they are invariably ruled by the Hindu Gods. Be it Christian, Muslim, or any other religious person, the life of all is decided in accordance with the Hindu Religion. That is to say, the virtuous deeds and sins of the people of this world are judged only in accordance with the Hindu Religion.

The Bible permits drinking alcohol, eating meat and even incestuous relationships with one's daughter or daughter-in-law. That is because men have created the Bible for their own convenience. But the Hindu *Vedas* (the principles of Hinduism) and the principles of humanitarian values, these are considered sins.

The Koran permits eating meat and marrying more than one woman. But as per the Vedas given to us by the Gods, a man is to marry only once. It is a sin to lust after another man's wife. The Koran permits all these acts because it was written keeping man's convenience in mind.

Whether the Christians abide by the Bible or the Muslims abide by the Koran, in the Christian and Islamic nations sounds of battlefields, bombing and people wailing have been renting the air for ages. People live in a constant state of fear and absence of peace because they do not abide by Hindu Vedas and Hindu Dharma.

Is God Murderous by Nature?

Both Christianity and Islam endorse spreading their respective religions and the eliminating of people who do not accept their religious doctrines. The Bible and the Koran assert that Jesus and Allah created all the men in this universe. But then how can the Creator sanction the killing of men whom He had created in the first place? And how can we say He is God?

Only a Being who shows mercy to all creatures can be revered as God. Hinduism demands that man should not harm even lowly insects like ants and flies and that he should be kind to all living creatures.

On 14 February 2019, in a place called Pulwama in Kashmir, in India, a suicide bomber killed forty paramilitary soldiers. In the video recorded before committing this heinous murder, the terrorist says that he will go to heaven as a reward for performing this terrorist act! If taking many lives guarantees a passage to heaven, won't men start committing mass murders in the hope of going to heaven and convert the world into a slaughterhouse? Forget murderers going to heaven; with repeated murders, won't the world turn into hell? Can a merciful God grant heaven to a man who kills others in order to gain a passage to heaven for himself?

It is a sin to commit murders to follow a religious path. In their ignorance, Christians and Muslims have been committing sins for hundreds of years. This is also the reason people across the globe are leading a life without peace of mind and remain afflicted by agitations, civil wars, struggles, terrorism, murders, dacoity, rapes and the fury of nature.

Okay. India is not an Islamic country. If a terrorist activity is conducted against India, the perpetrator goes to heaven. On 13 February, a Pakistani outfit called Jaish-al-Adl carried out a suicide attack in Iran and killed twenty-seven Iranian soldiers – that too

Muslim soldiers! Is heaven guaranteed even if one murders people who follow one's own religion?

It is possible to assert firmly that no other people except Indians know what is calmness of mind, peacefulness and happiness. Those who follow other religions equate carnal pleasures with inner happiness.

4

ONE'S ACCUMULATED VIRTUES SAVE ONE'S FUTURE GENERATIONS

The Indian people know an incantation which says 'One's accumulated virtues save one's future generations'. If the parents do good deeds, lead a virtuous life, stick to the right path, help others, have good conduct, their future generations will lead a blissfully happy life. If the parents' life is contrary to this, they will witness their offsprings' miseries and agonies and shed tears in helplessness.

This is the reason Indians have lived a life of virtue and good deeds for ages. India also remained a land of plenty. But things changed after the Christians and Muslims invaded our country, and Indians accepted religious conversions, forgot the dictum 'accumulated virtue protects one's future generations' and indulged in sinful deeds. Hence, Indians too, like the people of other countries, live without peace of mind or happiness. We witness painful incidents like murders, dacoity, rape, immorality, turmoil and terrorism.

Atheists Pose a Grave Danger

As per UNO's count of religious people, out of the world population of 730 crores, 230 crores are Christians. But in Christian countries, 80 per cent of the population are non-believers. Therefore, Muslims who are 130 crores are the highest number of religious people, Hindus are in second place,115 crores, and other religions, 85 crores. Thus, religious people are 494 crores in number while the rest of the world population are not followers of any religion.

What differentiates man from animals is his faith in God, humane qualities and his virtues. Animals do not have faith in God or the capacity to think. It is dangerous for the world to have a large majority of its population without faith in God.

5

THERE IS NO SUCH THING AS HINDU RELIGION!

People of all religions in the world and even those who deny the existence of God should lead a life guided by the divine scripture. That is the only way to find happiness and world peace. There is no need for Christians and Muslims to convert to Hinduism. Because there is no such religion as Hinduism – there never was! When the people of the world followed a particular religion, they identified those who worshipped a Supreme Being as 'Hindus'. The Hindu religion has remained evergreen despite six hundred years of Muslim rule, three hundred years of Christian rule, and now the attempt to crush Hinduism in the name of secularism because Hinduism shows the only genuine way to worship God.

How does one learn about Hinduism, its scriptures, puranas, epics and shastras?

Hinduism remains within the confines of India or is trapped in the countries that follow other religions. Out of the world population of 730 crores, 75 per cent of people are clueless about the religion called Hinduism, who is the genuine God or what are *Vedas* and puranas. Hinduism has never attempted to spread itself by advertising. But the people of the world should be told about Hinduism, God and the *Vedas*.

One way to do this is to ensure that this book of mine is widely read. Then see what happens after that!

Fine. The People of the world are eager to learn about Hinduism, God and the *Vedas*. How do we go about explaining these to them? Is it possible to translate the Rig Veda, Yajur Veda, Saama Veda, Atharva Veda, the Ramayana, the Mahabharata, Periya Puranam, religious texts like the Naalaayira Divya Prapandham into all the languages of the world and make printed copies? Does anyone know how many languages there are in the world? Even if the Vedas, puranas, epics and the shastras are translated into all the languages of the world, translation may rob some of the original meaning and beauty of the text. We need capable people to translate all these texts into the world languages, and it is a time-consuming process.

Spread the Tamil Language for People to Learn about Hinduism

There is a simple method to make the people of the world learn about Hinduism, God, the Vedas and religious treatises. Yes, spread the Tamil language across the globe. All the religious treatises are either in Sanskrit or in Tamil. No one speaks Sanskrit in the world. But Tamil is spoken all over the world. Once people learn Tamil, they will voluntarily read and internalise the Vedas, puranas and devotional treatises.

May the UNO be disbanded and let the people of the world follow the Hindu religion. Then there will be complete peace and happiness across the world.

The End